BE
DRAG
Fabulous

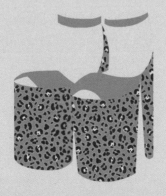

BE
DRAG
Fabulous

HOW TO LIVE YOUR BEST DRAG QUEEN LIFE

WRITTEN BY
QUEEN LAGRANDE

ILLUSTRATED BY
KATIE MOCKRIDGE

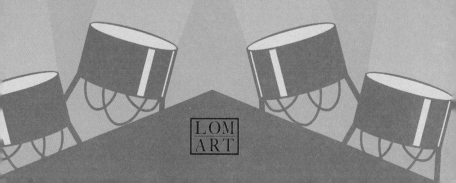

LOM
ART

Illustrations by
Katie Mockridge

First published in Great Britain in 2021 by LOM ART, an imprint of
Michael O'Mara Books Limited
9 Lion Yard
Tremadoc Road
London SW4 7NQ

A CIP catalogue record for this book is available from the British Library.

Papers used by Michael O'Mara Books Limited are natural, recyclable
products made from wood grown in sustainable forests. The manufacturing
processes conform to the environmental regulations of the country of origin.

ISBN: 978-1-912785-46-9 in hardback print format

ISBN: 978-1-912785-47-6 in ebook format

1 2 3 4 5 6 7 8 9 10

Designed by Barbara Ward

Printed and bound in China

www.mombooks.com

MIX
Paper from
responsible sources
FSC® C010256

FSC
www.fsc.org

To all the drag queens around the world, you are fierce and fabulous

Contents

Introduction

Drag queens are confident, slick and sassy, and they
don't live by other people's rules. They keep their
standards high and their heels higher. They work hard
and they laugh at themselves. They are lionhearted
yet sensitive, vocal yet vulnerable, charismatic and
colourful; they are balls of sparkle in a world of drab.
And now we can take a look at the tricks of the trade
and learn some lessons on life from the very best.

With over fifty positive and fun bits of advice to help you
follow in the heels of drag queens and apply their rules to
your everyday life, you'll be feeling the fantasy and serving
hotness wherever you go. Drag performances aren't just
an act for the stage, they are also all about personas we
take on as we boss every area of our lives. Being a queen
means being part of the influencing art form of drag
culture, and this responsibility is taken very seriously.

Their mantra is no matter your age, size, colour or ability, you can be whatever you want to be. There is no fear here, no failure, just inspiring lessons to show you that confidence is a way of life . . . and it's all for the taking, hunny.

Queens are willing to show both vulnerability and strength, and their rules for life will show you how to boss it and not let your crown slip in whatever you do. Stride onto their runway and learn how to free your inner desires, find your tribe and sissy your walk down your own path. Con*drag*ulations, darlings; it's time to be fabulous.

Time to take control and get positive: your
beautiful self won't get anywhere being
bitter or frustrated. Get back on track,
adjust your crown and remember who
you are. And enjoy every sassy step . . .

IT'S YOUR TIME TO SHINE

The key to shining is understanding when the spotlight is upon you. There is no need to feel frustrated if you don't think you're getting anywhere, darling; just own every decision you make and find your fire. In the same way you can't force yourself into a VIP club without an invite, make sure you focus on the end goal, even if you have to wait a while. Take a leaf out of Alaska's book; she auditioned for every single season of *RuPaul's Drag Race* before finally getting her chance to shine in season five. And she hasn't looked back. Ultimately, she is just a girl who decided to go for it, so be patient with your passion and you too will be rewarded when it's your time to shine.

ALASKA

YOU ARE
fabulous

You are a big ball of stupendousness, dipped in glitter and covered in awesomeness. You don't have to question your fabulousness; you suck it in like oxygen and radiate it from the tip of your beehive down to the sole of your eight-inch stilettos. The key to your fabulousness is that even though there might be fleeting moments when someone calls your splendour into question, you'll simple shrug it off, adjust your crown and remind whoever is challenging your marvelousness just who the hell it is they are dealing with. Being fabulous and knowing it isn't an attitude; it's a standard. And you have your standards permanently set to high.

TAKE RISKS
EVERY DAY

Have you heard the one about the drag queen making a risky choice, falling flat on her beautifully painted face and not getting up again? Nope, us neither. You live and breathe risk-taking because you were not put on this earth to stand still and be miserable. Taking a chance and rolling the dice is all about colour, passion, motivation, resilience and thrills. Avoiding risks in life is being beige – and drag queens just don't do beige. From now on you will take a risk every day and feel the fantasy. Otherwise you will lose the chance. Be the epitome of 'sickening', engage in the seemingly impossible and leave everyone awestruck at your bravery. Shoulders back, tits and teeth out and go.

GET YOUR
S**T
TOGETHER

It's time to woman up and get yourself into gear. We all have moments of self-doubt but that doesn't mean you fall apart at the first hurdle. Take a leaf out of Bob the Drag Queen's book and let the world know you are the shiniest cherry on top and proud of it. His mum always told him he could do anything, which instilled such a sense of self-worth in young Bob that she grew up telling the world how amazing she is. His mum believed in him, he believed in himself and nothing else mattered. You are frickin' fabulous so know your worth and get your s**t together. End of.

BOB THE DRAG QUEEN

BE THE JUDGE OF

everything

The fairy godmother of drag, RuPaul, has brought the world a million spiritual insights that make us not only follow her guidance but also want to live by her mantras. Being the judge of everything, the Queen of Judges herself places the emphasis on your own unique take on life. If something isn't right for you, change it. If someone doesn't float your boat, ditch them. Repeat in your head, 'I'll be the judge of that.' Adjudicate over everything and anything that comes into your life and make sure yours is the only voice you hear. Well, unless it's RuPaul's – then bow down to the head honcho.

RUPAUL

INSULTS ARE
water off a
DUCK'S BACK

Never has a mantra held more sway than Jinkx Monsoon's famous utterance. The American queen wasn't about shunning shade; she faced critique, accepted it and then let it roll off her just as the metaphor suggests. For Jinkx, it was an easier way of saying that it's not about her as a human being, as it wasn't a personal attack. And when she realized that it was an opportunity to improve rather than automatically piling on an emotional response, she was released from the venom of an insult. In the same way former First Lady Eleanor Roosevelt told us that 'No one can make you feel inferior without your consent,' First Lady of Drag Jinkx tells us to not give a duck.

JINKX MONSOON

Shantay
EVERY DAY

You are here to stay. There is no failure, no exit, no losing;
you are shantaying every single day. Once that is in the
forefront of your mind, it's time to work on spreading that
enchantement in every possible way (from the French word
'*enchanter*', which means to weave a bewitching spell).
You will be too much for some people but remember,
queen, those aren't your people and they can sashay away.
Walk into any situation with an entrance sparkle that will
dazzle and show that you are ready to own everything.

Never complain,
NEVER EXPLAIN

What better motto to live by than this gem from the Queen herself, the unofficial mantra of the royal family. Curtsy to the high standard that all queens should live by: never throw unnecessary shade and never feel like you owe strangers an explanation for anything you do. People will talk, read you to filth, gossip, assume and gawp anyway, no matter how you try to justify yourself. But the good news is: you don't have to care. It's your life, live it how you choose and whoever wants to talk about you will talk about you whether you like it or not. Complaining is cheap and nasty, so leave it to the cheap and nasty.

CRYSTAL, BLU HYDRANGEA, GOTHY KENDOLL AND SUM TING WONG

LAUGH
AT YOURSELF

Good ol' orphan Annie told us that we're never fully dressed without a smile, and that curly-haired redhead nailed it. If you can find fun and laughter in the small and silly things in your daily life and chuckle at yourself on a regular basis, then surely you're halfway there. Baga Chipz is the first to poke fun at herself – she even chose her name after a cheeky jibe from a guy in a bar when he referred to her as being common as muck. So take full advantage of any opportunity to chortle merrily when things go wrong because if you can't laugh at yourself, you're just giving someone else the opportunity to do it. Remember to laugh at the haters, too – just make sure they see the 'f**k you' in your giggle.

BAGA CHIPZ

ALWAYS HAVE YOUR
one-liners READY

Never one to disappoint her audience, Jujubee is the
queen who will always have the last word. She loves long
walks on the beach, fried chicken, and . . . other things.
Delivering hilarious one-liner after one-liner when she
appeared on *RuPaul's Drag Race*, she's a walking, talking
quotable queen. And the delivery of her sassy quips
is always perfectly executed. So, make sure you keep
some fierce one-liners at the back of your mind for
every occasion and be prepared to drop some verbal
fire into any conversation. The saltier the better.

JUJUBEE

Learn to celebrate and embrace what
people love about your magical soul and
become a more passionate, courageous
creature by following your heart. You should
never apologize for being enthusiastic
and unconditional with your love.

LABELS
DON'T MATTER

Labels can be great for finding yourself and your people, but they should never feel restrictive, and you should never be afraid to swap one label for another if you change your mind! Kiss whoever the hell you want, wear whatever the f**k you want and enjoy whatever it is that floats that glitter boat of yours. If we welcome all sizes, all colours, all cultures, all genders, all beliefs, all ages, all people, all we are doing is welcoming love. Of course, some people will still want to stick their own label on you, but peel it off. It was never that sticky in the first place.

Love Yourself

The one mantra that RuPaul is best known for, her closing statement at the end of each episode of *Drag Race*, is a reminder to us all that loving yourself comes first. One of the most beloved queens in *her*story, Cheryl Hole, is a good example to us all that making sure you have the utmost respect and love for yourself is where it's at. Regardless of what anyone feels about her, she chooses to love herself daily. Even when she is feeling 'mediocre'. Live like that, darlings, and be a shining beacon of self-adoration.

CHERYL HOLE

FREE YOUR
inner desires

Reaching your full potential means striving for something and focusing on it more than you have ever done in your life, because unless you can believe the future can be better, you are unlikely to make it so. There is no dream or desire too grand for any queen to achieve. No pessimist ever discovered the secrets of the stars, so let others throw shade your way, smile and nod but then damn well do whatever the hell you want. Do it again and again. We only get one life; it's time to make the most of it and free your inner desires.

SASHA VELOUR

Find someone who isn't intimidated by YOUR PERSONALITY

If ever there was someone to explain this lesson in a way that will have you pausing for breath, Divina De Campo is your gurl. She was quick to tell the other contestants on *RuPaul's Drag Race UK* how f**king fabulous she is when she asked if anyone else could sing in five languages and do the splits at the same time. She wore her talents with pride and her skills as her armour and if you too are all about your positivity, you will only attract good folks. So, find someone who won't run a mile at your chutzpah and rule the world together.

DIVINA DE CAMPO

PUT YOURSELF OUT THERE

As a self-confessed fat kid who had a strong lisp, Kim Chi classed herself as an outsider when she was younger. But although she struggled with self-confidence as a child, she hasn't let her past dictate her future. When you act determined, you feel determined – and putting yourself in situations where there is nowhere to hide means that everything you were afraid of exposing is now out there. And you know what? That fear of putting yourself out there has suddenly vamooshed because you *are* out there. And – shock, horror – the world hasn't stopped turning.

KIM CHI

FOCUS ON YOUR
ASSETS

If you are too busy working on your own grass, you won't notice if someone else's is greener. Which is exactly how it should be. The key to this message is to focus and appreciate what you have right in front of you. Failure, fear and courage are your greatest assets. Failure, because it gives you a chance to reset what you want from life. Fear, because it prompts you to get excited about something, if you learn to channel your fears in the right way. Courage, because you will overcome anything with it. And finally you need to top it all off with killer heels, because success is not giving a flying f**k when you are standing tall in your crown.

LOVE YOUR
WARTS
and all

Channel your inner Cheddar Gorgeous and live by her mantra – accept what was given to you and make it work. She escaped her normality when she was younger and immersed herself in a sci-fi world, watching *Star Trek* and finding solace in its fantastical queerness. The characters brought another dimension into her sheltered world and she found a kinship with their uniqueness. In essence, if you embrace a sense of peculiarity then you never have to define your drag look. Accept that we are all different and bring on the kookiness. Resistance is futile.

CHEDDAR GORGEOUS

Friendships

Navigating life without your soul sisters
by your side is like fixing your hair without
spray – it just doesn't work. So take time to
learn how to ditch the haters, rally with your
tribe and empower the next generation.

BE HONEST
WITH YOUR FRIENDS

Not to be confused with throwing shade, this honesty
comes from the need to protect and support your
fellow queens. It's not vicious or obnoxious commentary
(even by drag standards that's ugly); it's about helping
those in need . . . whether it's telling them to look at
how orange they look or that they're giving off a hot-
mess vibe. Or letting them know they've stepped
out without false eyelashes. Be a solidarity sister but
remember that a little friendly critique goes a long way.
Don't waste your time on cattiness, shallow-jibes or
snarky sneers. Kindness, kids – it goes a long way.

BE AN
ALLY

Showing solidarity to your sisters is always in fashion; be the relatable queen who spreads the language of acceptance, individuality and sparkle. Ynel Regalo won her Holland's Best Drag Queen title with a performance of the song 'Proud', unfurling an LGBTQ+ banner as she lip-synced. Getting the audience emotional, her message was loud and clear. Be like Ynel and fight for the upcoming queens, the ones unsure how they will fit in, the ones just starting out, the ones feeling lost. Don't be neutral, don't be beige, don't be quiet; now is the time to be vocal. Your open-mindedness is what is changing the world.

YNEL REGALO

NEVER BE AFRAID
to show vulnerability

Not to be confused with weakness, showing vulnerability
is the same as showing the world you aren't afraid to fail.
Remember that ol' chestnut from RuPaul – you know,
and the rest is drag? Know yourself, your rhythm, your
vibe and project it to the world. Growing up in a Paris
suburb where LGBTQ+ acceptance was hard to find,
Freya Kor found affection among the audience at her
drag shows. By embracing her imperfections, she created
a space where others felt safe to be themselves, too.
And it proved there was drag for everyone in the city.

FREYA KOR

CALL
shade

Those who throw shade need to be called out. Pointing out the lies and the nastiness is just about standing up and not being afraid to fight the feisty. You can have a fabulous tribe but there will always be one person who likes to ruffle your feathers. Woman up and call them on it. American queen Naomi Smalls insists that the reason she sleeps well at night is because she knows she's not a malicious person and she won't stand for any negativity or wrongdoing. So take a leaf out of Ms Smalls' book and don't be afraid to call 'Shade!' when you see it and to tell people to get out.

NAOMI SMALLS

FIND YOUR
TRIBE

It's easy to feel alone, outcast and teetering on the edge of society. But once you find people who share your passions and enthusiasms, you'll never walk in heels alone. Seek out and surround yourself with like-minded folk, find comfort in them and be inspired, motivated and entertained by them. Remember to make your weird light shine bright so other weirdos know where they can find you. And when they do, applaud their quirks with cries of 'Yes, me too!' Take on a mother or father role in that family and teach and inspire upcoming queens to hold their heads high and their crowns straight. Ask for advice and help whenever you need it and return it in abundance. Remember: the strength of the tribe is the queen and the strength of the queen is the tribe.

ACCEPT OTHERS'

quirks

Know what makes you *you* and accepting others will become second nature. Be in awe of the quirky, love the weird and wacky, and accept the crazy. Some of the kindest souls have the kookiest attributes and some of the most bizarre behaviours deserve to be celebrated. Remind yourself that just as your personality and peculiarities should be applauded and not simply tolerated, so you should do the same for others. Stay free in your authenticity; be your genuine, nice, silly, sarcastic, eccentric self and accept the quirky quality of others. Remember that every human on this planet is ridiculous in their own way and so you shouldn't judge or mock because at the end of the runway, none of it really matters.

DISH THE

Spilling the T is an essential bonding experience for queens; there's nothing better than a good gossip with a good friend (as long as it's not mean-spirited, of course). Gossip brings people together and the more piping hot the tea, the better. Spilling the T at every opportunity also teaches the new generation of queens to be strong, powerful and pay those b**ches no mind.

MONÉT X CHANGE & NAOMI SMALLS

BE *seen,*
BE *heard*

Put your stamp on the world by raising your voice and raising your standards – it's all about letting people hear you and see you and what you stand for. Channel your inner Yoncé Banks, Beyoncé's biggest fan, and live by her words of acceptance and understanding. She believes that you will never appreciate different kinds of people if you fail to respect them and their differences. The way you treat people speaks volumes about who you are, so treat them well and be heard. A lady should always be seen and heard, so remember: loud and proud, darling. Loud and proud.

YONCÉ BANKS

WERK, WERK, WERK

Boss ladies don't get anywhere in life without the right attitude and unstoppable focus, so it's time to set your sights on building your empire. Good things come to those who werk, so just keep killin' it, as always.

DON'T LET OTHERS HOLD YOU BACK

Paving his own yellow brick road hasn't been easy for Todrick Hall. When he started out in the entertainment business, he was told that the worst thing he could ever be in this world is a black gay man. But he was determined to overcome such bigoted attitudes, and while LGBTQ+ artists still don't get the billings and recognition that they deserve, Todrick wants to see change. He knows that many talented people don't believe they can do something because they have never seen anybody who looks like them do it before, and Todrick also knows that is the exact reason they should be doing it. Amen to that.

TODRICK HALL

EXCUSES ARE FOR LOSERS.
Own a failure

Queens don't quit – they get up, adjust their crown and start all over again. Literally, in Adore Delano's case, when she tried to stage-dive into a crowd during a Pride celebration in Canada. The crowd parted and she fell right through them, scraping her knee. Did she throw a hissy fit? Did she stop performing for her fans? Did she hell! She shrugged, she made a sarcastic comment, she carried on. Failing, even in that small sense, is about learning. Failure is never, ever the end of the road. Read that again, please, ladies. Failure is the big pink feather boa waving to you, saying, 'Wrong way, b**ch. Just turn around and keep going!'

ADORE DELANO

Change
DIRECTION
if you need to

Like not being afraid to fail, being adaptable is basic drag 101. It's never too late to shed your skin and reset your goals, refocus and readjust as many times as you need to. You are the queen of reinventing, of creation, and when it comes to paving the way and finding your direction, aim high or go home. The biggest mistake you can make is to not realize the sky is the limit. Have a never-ending list of goals and follow your heart because it will lead you to where you need to be. Now hold onto your wig and off you go, babe!

JUNO BIRCH

BE BOLD
AND *go for it*

American queen Jan makes no apologies for her unflinchingly ambitious nature – for her, it's part and parcel of creating a persona in order to achieve something. Mama Ru is often pushing for the daring and brave, and Jan is the epitome of what being bold is all about. She is ambitious, she is driven and she doesn't apologize for it. But don't confuse ambition with execution. Thinking ambitious thoughts but actually being ambitious are two different things. You have to get s**t done and not let your fears overtake your goals. You either live with the pain of something not working (you fall down, you get your sorry ass back up again) or the pain of regret (you've lost your chance). Ain't nobody want to feel that pain.

JAN

BECOME THE HARDEST WORKING PERSON YOU KNOW

Way back in 2003, Shane Jenek auditioned for *Australian Idol*. He didn't make the cut so he came back the next day as Courtney Act and her drag act blew away the judges. As the first openly LGBTQ+ contestant to appear on any reality show in the world, this was a queen who was going to work hard to get where she wanted. Courtney not only paved a way for others like her to audition for mainstream reality shows, she also went on tour, signed a record deal, appeared in more TV shows, became the first drag queen to perform live with the San Francisco Symphony Orchestra and appeared in a major American ad campaign. Stick that in your pipe and smoke it, darling!

COURTNEY ACT

Success
DOESN'T COME
WITHOUT
sacrifice

You won't find a queen who hasn't sacrificed something
along the glittery path to success, so don't expect things
to fall into place without drama. Physical, financial and
personal sacrifice is commonplace if you want to garner
attention in this extravagant world. Sacrifice everything and
anything to get where you want to be and don't let your fear
of looking like a d*ck hold you back. As one queen once said,
'Be unapologetic . . . even if it means sacrificing everything.'

YOU'RE NEVER TOO *old* TO *try*

As we get older, we tend to give less of a f**k about what people think, which makes a vintage queen full of wisdom, life experience and a hell of a lot of couldn't-give-a-damn. So gird your loins and go forth and sparkle because there is no set age for anything in this life. If you can wear sequins on your eyelids, like big hair and big heels, you're halfway there. Just ask Aquaria, who won season ten of *RuPaul's Drag Race*. OK, so she was the youngest queen to take part that season at just twenty-one years old, but you know, it's all the same thing. In a nutshell, as soon as you feel too old to do something, that's when you should do it.

AQUARIA

WALK YOUR OWN PATH

Growing up in Belfast, Northern Ireland, there wasn't exactly an abundance of stages for Blu Hydrangea to perform on when she first started drag – in fact, there were just two gay bars opposite each other on one street. But instead of letting this extinguish her flamboyant flame, she took to Instagram and YouTube and forged a new path for herself to showcase her blooms. Because when a flower isn't flourishing, you fix the conditions, not the flower itself. Isn't that right, petal?!

BLU HYDRANGEA

USE YOUR
FLAWS
AS YOUR
STRENGTHS

As a wise queen once said, 'F**k this s**t' – and then she lived happily ever after. No matter what situation you are in, someone can always throw shade on you and the key to not losing your cool is to not give a rat's ass. Own everything, even your real-life hindrances, and turn them into your drag superpower . . . and ta-dah! No one can use them against you. Use fashion and beauty to amp up your queendom and be proud to expose and use your flaws as part of your armour.

Self-care

Taking time to focus on yourself, get your sass back on track and replenish your sense of self-worth is the most valuable investment you will ever make. Never skip this step in life, ever.

Not today, Satan

Winner of *RuPaul's Drag Race* season six, Bianca Del Rio
served up this iconic line when she was on the show and
we have been repeating it ever since. Simply translated,
one day you might screw it all up, but not today! Just
mutter Bianca's mantra every morning when you wake
up and you'll be certain to see off any devilish crap that
might dare to get in your way – because, let's face it,
you don't have the time for any nonsense today, or any
other day, for that matter. Flaunt that message loud
and clear: the devil won't be stealing any souls today!

BIANCA DEL RIO

PLUS SIZE
is positive

Just because you're a bigger girl doesn't mean you can't
be a diva – just ask Latrice Royale, one of America's
most beloved queens. She is, in her own words, 'chunky
yet funky' and celebrates that fact – she doesn't give
a damn about what others think of her size. She lives
for showing off her swerves and curves and we love her
most for bringing such positivity into our lives. After
all, it doesn't matter how tall you are or what shape and
size you are, so long as the glitter in your soul, strength
of your character and size of your heart are all XXL.

LATRICE ROYALE

Pretty ISN'T EVERYTHING

Bimini Bon-Boulash is the sort of queen who doesn't put much stock in the idea of pretty. Her best make-up tip is to simply take photographs from a distance. Not a joke, just a fact. And isn't that refreshing? Whoever said beauty is on the inside was, let's face it, probably no oil painting, but it's time to accept that being pretty isn't actually the whole kit and caboodle. Being bold, being fearless, being a badass who knows what she wants in life is a whole lot more desirable and attractive than just being a pretty painted face.

BIMINI BON-BOULASH

WE ALL HAVE
BAGGAGE

Name a queen who doesn't have a tear-jerking *her*story, a heartbreaking experience or a troublesome chapter in their lives and we will show you a liar. Of course, we all have our own baggage, our own fears and worries and backstories, but unless you are the face of Louis Vuitton's latest luxury luggage range, baggage doesn't make you special. We've all got baggage; it makes us who we are. You need to decide whether to trip over it or unpack it, but whatever you do, own it. No queen has ever left it at baggage reclaim.

Dance your cares away

Dropping your hips onto the stage so hard the building shakes might not be a physician-recommended dance move, but it certainly goes to show that Katya Zamolodchikova isn't afraid to hit the dancefloor for all its worth. The American queen, who knows the importance of taking care of her mental health, appreciates the mood-lifting merits of a good shimmy so even if your gyrating, stumbling, swaying moves aren't as fierce as other queens, just turn up the volume wherever you are and let loose. Never, we repeat, *never* miss a chance to throw some shapes.

KATYA ZAMOLODCHIKOVA

CELEBRATE
WHAT MAKES
YOU DIFFERENT

Some people might want you to keep your crazy hidden away, but what exactly will that prove? That you're not different? Or that you're just good at hiding your true self? Everybody is weird, sweetheart, and you won't find a single queen who doesn't celebrate that fact and embrace their individuality. The moment you let embarrassment set in or become ashamed of your quirks, you lose your magic. You are inimitable and that is your superpower.

Confidence

IS A WAY OF

LIFE

It's time to stop thinking that confidence is something we need to dredge up in any given situation – queens don't get ready, they stay ready. They have no time for timidity or nerves and they wear confidence like they wear make-up – layer upon layer of it. It's not something that comes and goes; it's a way of life. Queens are walking, talking examples of confidence and self-assurance and, when surrounded by other queens, they feed off the atmosphere of that conviction. Bashful b**ches don't get anywhere, so be a confident queen!

DON'T LIVE BY
other people's
RULES

It's often said you should make your own kind of music but Trixie Matell doesn't just do her own thing – she flouts the rules at any given opportunity. For her, it's not about sticking to the tame, the harmless, the tried-and-tested performances; it's about pushing the boundaries and breaking the rules. She isn't one to play it safe and adhere to society's codes. Where's the fun in that? Controversial queens rarely give a damn and nor should you.

TRIXIE MATELL

THE SHOW
must GO ON!

They say that you can't keep a good woman down and The Vivienne, who won the first season of *RuPaul's Drag Race UK*, is a queen who won't let anything stand in her way. Not even a global pandemic. When Covid-19 threatened the drag scene, with performances cancelled and clubs closed, things looked pretty bleak. But The Viv was quick to spread the word about staying positive and not dwelling on the negative. She told her fans that the best thing to do was to take each day as it comes and remember that everyone was in the same boat. Show of hands – who else wants to be in The Viv's boat?!

THE VIVIENNE

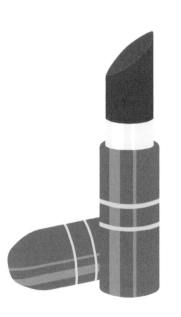

BEAUTY AND *Fashion*

If you can remember to dress to impress
every single day and understand that beauty
is an attitude, you will go far in this world.
Bring glamour, colour and exuberance
to your hair, make-up and clothes, and
leave a trail of sparkle in your wake.

The *bigger* THE HAIR, the *better*

If another queen drags you for your hair being 'too big', ditch the b**ch right away. You don't need that kind of negativity in your life. Big hair equals big dreams. Just like your eyelashes, which should be long and voluminous, big hair speaks volumes about the standards you keep. It shouldn't just be blocking *a* view; your gravity-defying wig is *the* view. The bigger the hair, the more people stare and when all else fails with a #look, just make the hair higher. 'My hair is too big,' said no queen ever.

CO-ORDINATE, CO-ORDINATE, CO-ORDINATE

With yourself, with you friends, with your passions. It's how you look sickening on a daily basis because your look and your style go hand-in-hand with your personality. You turn the party with your look and your vibe is an art form. Drag, darling, has forever led the way in the world of high fashion; designers are always keeping a beady eye on the avant-garde world of drag. Inspire the next generation of queens with your co-ordinated looks that reflect *you* and bring storytelling into your style.

Sparkle! Sparkle! Sparkle!

Just twenty-one years old when she entered *RuPaul's Drag Race*, Gigi Goode was all about the sparkle. Polished from head-to-toe, Gigi made sure all that glittered was Goode and spread her sparkle on every challenge. Sequins weren't just on her clothes and glitter wasn't just on her eyelids – it also ran through her veins so that she shone from within. So, if you need a little encouragement to dazzle, think Gigi and add more sparkle, more twinkle, more glitter and more spark wherever you go. A queen who leaves a trail of glitter is never forgotten.

GIGI GOODE

THE ANSWER
IS *always*
HAIRSPRAY

Hairspray is your lifeline. All hair needs help, especially gravity-defying, three-foot-high wigs. Investing in your hair is always worthwhile: hairspray really will hold your life together. Share it and spread the love, spray before you play and may your convictions and your desires be always as strong as your hair. If everything else falls apart around you, at least you won't have a strand out of place.

Slay THAT look

Canadian-born queen Crystal isn't afraid to mess
with boundaries when it comes to how she looks. She
doesn't believe drag is just about 'looking like a woman',
whatever that means: it's about playing with gender, being
experimental and not conforming to expectations. Crystal
slays her own individual look and because she competes with
no one when it comes to her style, no one can compete
with her. Her hair, make-up and clothes are always just
right – so follow her lead and make sure that any look you
go for is executed to perfection. Go for the look that fits
your personality, that suits your mood, that works with
your vibe and projects your attitude. Get ready to slay!

CRYSTAL

Feather boas are LIFE

Feather boas are an essential: you should never be caught without one on hand. Children love playing dress-up, and there is almost always a feather boa lurking in the dressing-up box, just waiting to add a glamourous edge to a young starlet. Your inner goddess should always be draped in a feather boa, even if your outer self isn't. In every possible situation, make an entrance like Mae West and sashay in with a boa draped around your neck – at least in your imagination. You'll never be overlooked in a boa . . .

Keep your HEELS and STANDARDS HIGH

Aerial hoop star Violet doesn't keep her feet on the ground (literally or metaphorically) when it comes to following her dreams; she makes sure her eyes are on the prize. How are you meant to live the high life if you are in flats? The higher the heel, the closer to God, as they say – and every click of your heels will remind you to own the ground you walk on. At over six feet tall, Violet, who has toured with burlesque star Dita Von Teese, knows all about putting her best high-heeled foot forward when it comes to fashion. Heels are life, ladies, and don't ever let your standards slip.

VIOLET CHACHKI

Look FIERCE, feel FIERCE!

Everyone struggles with confidence at some point in their lives, and you're not alone in facing criticism and doubts from other people. But hey, newsflash: drag queens teach us to forget the haters and use criticism to fuel your inner fierceness. Turn heads and drop jaws with your killer looks – looking fierce is all about *feeling* fierce. And don't ever let that fierce flame be extinguished: when you look fierce, you radiate fierce, you feel fierce. Confidence isn't an issue – not because you always feel it but because you are following in Alyssa Edwards' footsteps and you know how to overcome self-doubt. Be bold, be brash, be fierce!

ALYSSA EDWARDS

Index

GOTHY KENDOLL 27

JAN 75

JINKX MONSOON 23

JUJUBEE 30

JUNO BIRCH 72

KATYA ZAMOLODCHIKOVA 96

KIM CHI 42

LATRICE ROYALE 91

MONÉT X CHANGE 62

NAOMI SMALLS 57, 62

RUPAUL 20

SASHA VELOUR 38

SUM TING WONG 27

THE VIVIENNE 104

TODRICK HALL 68

TRIXIE MATELL 103

VIOLET CHACHKI 120

YNEL REGALO 53

YONCÉ BANKS 65

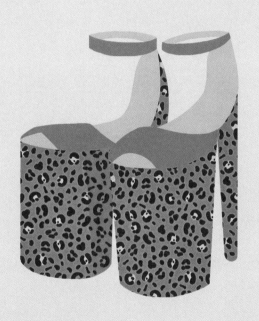